1

Preface

The subject for this novel is the Lucifer effect. Converting an ordinary, honest man to a sinister sadist.

The brilliant personality, the archangel Lucifer, was of the opinion that he is more outstanding then the other angels. When he, in his hubris, refuses to do God's will, God's anger, his sacred anger, transforms Lucifer to an unscrupulous devil - to the Devil himself.

This is the personality transformation an ordinary, honest public servant is subjected to the very same day he's employed as a prison guard. He becomes an evil person who lets the inmates feel his cruelty.

This is a novel, in the sense that I have used the writer's freedom to write – Licencia Poetica.

The persons or the personage in this novel are fictive.

In case you have comments, please, feel free to send a line to gunnar at barkenhammar dot nu

Enjoy your reading!

Gunnar Barkenhammar

Chapter 1.   Preludes

Pretty soon she will come out from the grocery store with her shopping bags, enter her car and drive home. And pretty soon she'll discover that she has a flat tire.

She has two alternatives. To call a garage for help on the spot or drive the short way home with a flat tire. In any case it will be an distraction in her peaceful living and not only for her, but also for her husband.

He remembered the beatings, the grin and the disgrace. It was penalty enough to be behind bars, but on top of that he and his inmates had the prison guards and their scorn, their disrespect.

Many times, he wondered why? Why behave cruelly as a prison guard? Or at least the ones he had met. And why become a prison guard? It wasn't that hard to get a decent work.

In any case she was driving home and very, very slowly and he followed her way back. She parked the car at the little parking place that belonged to the house. In a few hours her husband would come home and apply the spare tire. Then he would bring the car to a tire company. Then they could see that the valve had been cut off.

He did his first pinprick shortly after being released. Someone had thrown a bunch of flyers in a bush. He bought a tube of super glue and pretended to be an advertising distributor. At the mailbox of the prison guard he acted like he got a call on his cell phone. Protected behind his jacket he could glue the lid of the mailbox. It should take a hacksaw to open the mailbox. Why, they would ask themselves.

Chapter 2.   The Crime

Ten years old he had taken part in a robbery in a kiosk. A gang of guys same age triggered each other. By breaking a window, it was easy to get in. They found a few pennies and some candy.

The Police tracked them, and this burglary denounced them all for the rest of their lives.

Consequently, Gustav had problems getting a job after school. A farmer pitted him, and he could work as a farming hand. Milking the cows, drive the mower and things like that.

The farmer was a great fan of the fictional writer, the MP and the painter Mr. Gunnar Eriksson. Gunnar's sister Astrid was just writing books for children and Pippi Longstocking was just a crazy child.

Pippi was Astrid Lindgren's protest against the school system. This became obvious when Astrid got a German award for the best book of the year for children. The Germans wanted her to send her thank-you-speech in advance – well aware of the criticism of the German School system she would deliver. So, they answered that it will be totally sufficient for Mrs. Lindgren just say thank you. "I'm convinced that there are other writers well worthy of your award". Then Astrid Lindgren could deliver her speech.

Tolerance was part of Gustav's upbringing. Tolerance to those who had another opinion and tolerance to those who deviate from the established course. Later in life he could ask himself if one should be tolerant to those who were intolerant.

The number of women working outside home was low at the time. The women were housewives and the husbands' salary were sufficient to keep the families going.

In the Soviet economy 90% of the women were working outside home. There the position of the woman was different. She wasn't dependent of a husband to support herself and her children, while the Swedish woman was kind of hostage in her own home. Without her husband's salary she couldn't live. This characterized the order of command in the home.

Maybe the Lucifer process worked here as well. The husband supplied with the money and in a way, he had power over the wife. The concept of power can be defined as the one who has power over someone can force this someone to act contrary to his interests.

Regarding the family in the example above the power is money. Regarding the inmates the power is controlled by the society. The prisons have received resources to exercise power over the inmates. Power built on violence. The inmate is punished if he doesn't behave accordingly.

The more power, more sanctions the prison guards endorses against the inmates the less popular the prison guards will be. In the same way – the better the prison managers deliver their actions and decisions for the inmates the less problem with their popularity.

Gustav wasn't specifically devoted to the place where he was brought up. Many times, he wanted to be somewhere else. There must be other views than the municipality's. And the anonymity a bigger community offers.

After a six years elementary school Gustav's father Karl had few options to get a work. A solid day at the sawmill in the nearby village gave 25 ore. The parental home in Kalvsjömåla had extensive woodlands. A squirrel fur could be sold at 25 ore. Karl shoot three squirrels a day and made three time the salary of a sawmill worker.

As a seventeen-year-old he had enough money for a ticket to Chicago, where he could live at his elderly sisters Eleonora and Elisabeth.

His sister Eleonora got pregnant a little too early and was sent by her father Constantin to Chicago. Here Karl could attend the evening school and with a little knowledge in English he could work for the construction companies.

The stock market was booming during the 30th. After a few

years in the construction business he could work full time on the stock market. He became a very rich youngster.

He got engaged with the very charming Florence. During the Black Monday in 1929 he lost all his savings. Why he didn't anticipate the crash is a good question as he was very good at foreseeing what might happen.

Florence marries the chemist who created the toothpaste Crest. Many years later Florence and her reluctant husband visits Gustav hoping to see Karl.

Florence's husband is referring to his family originating from Switzerland as far back as the 14th century. Gustav realizes the poor man's situation and answers that his family cannot be traced that far back. We can only trace our family back to the 17th century when my ancestor Oluffs were fighting for king Sigismund at

Stångebro in 1598 together with his nephew Peder Mikaelson, who after the battle was knighted Hammarskiöld. The word Hammar comes from the lakes Hammar – both shaped as hammers - not far from Kalvsjömåla. That Gustav could trace his family back to Carl Martel who ruled France in the 9th century is a different story.

Karl had a remarkable sense for figures – a family trait with a good number of professors in mathematics. Gustav didn't have this mathematical trait, to Karl's disappointment.

The house manufacturer Standardhus had to run two shifts and they needed workers. Gustav was employed to nail parts for roofs.

With half a liter of vodka in his pocket Gustav went to the amusement park. The chief of the local police brought him home to his parents, who didn't find it strange that the son was drunk a Saturday evening. He was a good son. Fighting and drinking were typical during Saturday evenings at the amusement park. Ladies liquor – red as well as white – was for the upper class.

Vodka during Saturdays was as naturally as to drink milk during the weekdays. He never felt any need for alcohol, but it was kind of relaxing. One Saturday evening he went to Standardhus. The big border truck was easy to start. He emptied his vodka bottle as he was driving. Finally, he went into a board stack and there ended the Saturday pleasure. He got two years for drunk driving, which was to be served in Malmo.

Chapter 3.   The Time in Prison

" All penalties should serve as
improvements"
Olaus Petri in 1540.

Gustav went to the Police Station and
reported to the Mr. Albertsson, Local
Chief of the Police, who gave him a
railway ticket to Malmo. Personnel
from the Malmo penal institution would
meet him at Malmo Central. That
Gustav should escape, steal a car and
run away wasn't included in the
imaginary world of Mr. Albertsson nor
in Gustav's. Mr. Albertsson entrusted
Gustav that he considered two years
was just too much for what he had

done. Years later a Russian submarine was stranded far into the Swedish archipelago. The Russians didn't have to serve one single day for drunk driving. However, now it was as it was, when it didn't turn out the way it should, according to Mr. Albertsson's opinion.

The personal from the Malmo prison recognized Gustav when he disembarked the train.

When he checked in, he had to submit his personal belongings. He got institutional clothes and was assigned to a cell for the nights. During daytime he was supposed to work at the workshop and during his spare time he could play table tennis with the other inmates. They also had a small gym and a library. From Malmo library they could get just any book they wanted. The most popular book was "The Mafia" and also books about chemical experiments. We may wonder why. If you wanted to study, time was allocated for that. Regular time for breakfast, lunch and dinner was good for the health. However, the interior was meager. No flowers in the window shelves, no paintings on the walls, no plants. Which may have been good for the rehabilitation. He was very fond of playing table tennis. Maybe he played for one hour a day. There was always someone to play with. The inmates had a tournament where the looser had to give one SEK to the winner. At the workshop they earned 3 SEK an hour, so one SEK was quite a lot of money. Gustav was so good he was qualified to play in the Inmate Championship. Gustav went to Stockholm without any kind of surveillance. Here he met the real pros, those had been imprisoned for a long time and many times. He was down and out rather early in the tournament. But it was fun and a variety to the daily routines at the institution.

The inmates also wanted boxing and boxing instructions. Gustav disliked violence and left the lecture with headache as an excuse. He was of the definite opinion that boxing should be prohibited. It cannot be good for the brain to get permanent concussions. The brain cells die. Many boxers get boxing dementia, same as Alzheimers. To try to hit a human being unconscious is abuse and for sure no sport. And all this in front of a screaming audience.

The inmates also suggested a soccer game between the inmates and the prison guards. The institution management realized that the aim was to hurt the prison guards and to further escalate the conflicting relationship between the inmates and the prison guards. Shame on such an excellent opportunity, was the reaction from the inmates.

It is somewhat pathetical to read the statements from the prison management how they want to be identified:

- We cooperate for quality, efficiency, security and a positive affectioness. (with whom we can ask?)
- Our work brings our clients possibilities to development and change. We are clear and correct and good models.
- Our work with our clients is founded on knowledge, flexibility and empathy without waiving our integrity.
- We feel responsibility for and we are proud about our public mission and we are loyal to the purpose and the objective our mission.
- We feel committed and part of our work and we fully understand the

significance of our own work for the wholeness.

- We perform our work so the confidence for our institution is reinforced.

For sure in bright contrast to the reality. The institution wants to show a pretty facade, but with the rotten interior the façade crackles. It looks like a copywriter at an advertising agency has written the text.

Pretty soon Gustav realized there is a ranking in the prison. The crueler the crime the higher the rank. There was no secret who was in for what. It was the first thing the fellow inmates asked about. The truth wasn't questioned as it was easy to check at the court. All judges or sentences are official. The pedophiles had the lowest rank. And they were also punished by the other inmates. The risk for getting the pouch cut off was a reality for them.

It was amazing there was so many aliens among the inmates. Arabic was more or less the language spoken among the inmates. A good proof of the connection between the immigration and the crime. He picked up a few words: Jalla jalla, Bokra fil mich mich. Bedi nam mak.

The professionals belonged to a network of other criminals. After some time, he learned who belonged to which network. Every network had an inner circle who commanded the others in the network. The networks were enemies and fighting each other whenever they could. It was difficult to imagine that anyone in a network would leave the prison as good civilian judging from the language they used. The prison wasn't a good institution for rehabilitation for professional criminals. Nor for anyone detained in here. Sometimes Gustav felt like Günther Wallraff, writing notes in a notebook. It would be good to make a movie about the life in the prison, but he guessed not one single prison guard would like to show their family the kind of regiment they are running in the prison. Maybe he could make some kind of documentary when released.

That the Stockholm syndrome should work in the prison looked rather impossible. That the inmates should develop some kind of a relationship to the prison guards looked unreasonable. The relation between the prison guards and the inmates couldn't get worse. The criticism against the system had to take another course.

In the prison the inmates got to know each other, and they could widen their network. The prison was like a school for the criminals.

The local vicar, who visited the prison from time to time, was of the opinion that Gustav should stay away from the other inmates as far as he possibly could. The vicar also advised Gustav that in case he was called for a meeting with prison guards, he should ask someone of the other inmates to come along just not to be accused of slandering about something he had head.

Within the prison you were kind of encapsulated from the exterior world. The inmates could listen to radio, you could watch TV, and there were also newspapers and magazines, but still Gustav felt like he had lost 2 years of his life.

The inmates had fun with inserting an U-shaped wire in the power outlets, and thus short circuiting the electrical power. Part of the prison was darkened. Another fun was to trigger or activate the fire alarm. An inmate had spent a substantial amount of time to cut a tube for the radiators by a hacksaw blade. The hot water was flowing over the floor of the workshop.

Maybe this was a revenge of the system or maybe it was just an expression for idleness. Gustav was more and more convinced that this was not a way to create good citizens of the inmates. Rather the system created wicked citizens. For sure it wasn't an easy task to create a better system. You had to show that the retribution or reprisal was destructive instead of constructive. The friend of order would never accept a system without any kind of reprisal. Part of a solution is education and specifically professional education to enable the inmate to get a job and a fellowship in a working team. Construction work, car mechanic, restaurants, where there is teamwork. The education could take place at the working places with a GPS-surveillance. If robots could take care of our elderly a robot could be an inmate companion.

The first-time criminals like himself weren't too much of a problem, but what about the professionals. They don't want to and, in many cases, they just cannot break up from the group. The group pressure is strong. They serve the time just to get back in business. Here the key is the network. How to break the networks. Many times built from their childhood. In a free society just, anyone can socialize with whoever they want. On the other hand, there is a ban for perpetrators of violence, so consequently why not have a ban for criminal networks. The Police must be able to map the criminals in the networks. One other key could be to permanently have a GPS surveillance of the leaders in the criminal networks. Hells Angels and Bandidos should be easy. Here the criminality is the lifestyle. Tracking and trailing could prevent most of the crime. Same way with the other networks.

A radical handling would be to captive the professionals preventively, but now the law is like it is. We can punish someone for a crime he has committed but not for a crime he may commit. However, for terrorist crimes the intension is punishable, and then we can do the same way with our local terrorists. On top of this you can make the penalties progressive in the same way as we have our tax rates progressive. The better we are doing the higher the tax.

Then there are those mentally ill – pedophiles and rapists, pyromancies and kleptomaniacs. They should be brainwashed at a mental hospital, not detained in a prison. Then we have those who are incredibly irritable and then they become violent. Maybe there are some kind of medication to treat them. The prison wasn't a good medication for them. In the same way with the psychopaths. They have a good number of mental problems and the prison is not a good way to treat their problems.

In this way many prisons will be redundant and the prison guards jobless. That someone would employ an ex prison guard seemed Gustav as unreasonable as someone should employ and ex-convict. To find Sture jobless would be great. He was wondering how long Sture would follow him after his release, Sture occupied him quite a lot. For those like me, Gustav believed, it would be best to adjusted at home. In my case it was the alcohol even if I'm not an alcoholic. Those of the inmates who were in for alcoholism counted the days until they were released and could get drunk. In spite of the treatments they got in the prison.

The prison management
wanted the inmates to talk to people
outside the prison. Volunteers who
came for a short chat. Maybe they were
paid maybe not. In any case coffee and
cookies were served. Some came from
different congregations. Maybe they
thought they could get new followers,
maybe they just wanted to do
something good. Gustav tried to talk
about Jesus Christ as a wizard. How he
could walk on water, revoke the dead,
heal the lame. Not even the Superman
nor Mr. Walker could do that. And
what about the mathematics? The
Father, the Son and the Holy Ghost
must be three. But Christianity was of
the opinion that three was equal to one.

Maybe the idea with these
conversations was salvation. Alcoholics
can be cured by either falling in love or
be salved.

It isn't that easy to be
released from a prison. There are few

employers who want an ex-inmate. Thus, it is difficult to resist a quick fix. Within 2 years after the release more than half of the released inmates are convicted to a new sentence.

The prisoners were locked up a little too early in the evenings so the prison guards shouldn't have to work overtime. When they were denied leave, this was notified by mocking comments. How to make this public to the politicians and to the community? Maybe a letter to the editor or a public debate, but who to sign? For sure not an inmate.

After some time, it was difficult to differ one day from the other. Thanks to the radio he could take part of what was happening outside the walls. To pass time he started to study English over the net. Thus, he would be released as a better person according to the institution management.

- Ouch, why did you step on my foot? It hurts and very much so. I have gym shoes and you have boots.
- Oh dear, did I step on your foot? Keep your feet away they are sticking out from the cell.
- You did this volontarily.
- No way
- I want the institution doctor to take a look at my foot. I have a table tennis match tomorrow.
- Lay down on the bed and I'll lock you up.
- Ouch, now you jammed my fingers. How will this work tomorrow?
- Do you think I care?
- No, why should you
- Yes, why should I.

This was a punishment within the punishment. One other punishment was the seclusion in a cell maybe 2x3 m. In the bed there are leather straps.

Seclusion 23 hours a day with a break of one hour in an indoor yard. An inhuman punishment within the punishment. One other day Gustav witnessed how the prison guards abused an inmate who had been impertinent to them.

- What did you see, asked Sture
- Nothing
- I hope so and for eternity.
- I don't know what you are talking about
- Disappear and immediately
- Sure

Sture knocks Gustav with his baton.

- Ouch, you are not allowed to have such a baton.
- That's none of your business. Just disappear!

Abuse, seclusion and hard words on top the punishment they were serving. From that moment Gustav decided revenge. It wouldn't be too hard to find out where Sture lived. During the summers Malmo City offered entertainment almost every evening at the amphitheater in garden build after the Baltic exhibition in 1914. The entertainment started at 1900 h and lasted for one hour. A favorite during his leave.

During the leaves he wondered what to do after the release. Drive a cab, maybe. On the other hand, it didn't matter as long as he could support himself. To go back to the work at Standardhus was unthinkable, even if he could get it back.

He would stay in Malmo to get his revenge. The vicar had indicated that he might have a job for him.

When released he had both a job and an apartment in the inner part of Malmo.

Chapter 4.　　　　The Prison Guard

Working as an office worker wasn't especially fun nor well paid. When their daughter was about to start high school, they wanted her to live at home. Thus, he applied for a job in Malmo as a prison guard.

It was a little hard to break up from the little village where his father as well as his grandfather had worked at the local industry. Here he had his best friends and his network

He took school as something that had to be done. At school he wasn't one of the brightest, but he managed. He liked the military service and he considered to apply for the Police school. Working as a Police officer would be great, and the promotion regulated. He liked being dressed in a uniform. For one reason or another he didn't get admission to the Police School. The local industry wanted someone who could calculate the wages and that became his work.

He met his wife Mona at a public dancing hall. Mona was a beautiful lady and constantly invited to dance. She was a housewife. There weren't many work opportunities in the little village. In Malmo she managed to get a work as a shop assistant. She had no experience as a shop assistant, but she was well dressed and a true beauty, blond, blue eyed with pleasant manners.

The shop owner noted she could handle the clients and they trusted her judgement. She had that special feeling for colors and what was suitable. Her salary wasn't high, but a good supplement to the family. The price they had to pay for the little house they bought in Malmo was well over the price they got for the house they sold in the village, so each and every penny was badly needed.

They tried to keep in touch with the old friends from the village. Talking over the phone from time to time, but soon Sture realized that his new profession wasn't appreciated. In a way he felt slightly isolated. To find new friends in Malmo wasn't easy, and their company was the colleagues - Mona's and to his.

Mona attended a course in English. Some English she knew from school. She also got new girlfriends. She appreciated the big city with shopping malls, restaurants and coffee shops. She felt at home.

At the English course she got to know a lady from Cameroon. She was from the French speaking part of Cameroon, and now she learned some

English. After the course had finished, they went for a cup of coffee. Alice, as her name was, was a stimulating acquaintance with a catching laugh.

Mona and Sture appreciated Malmo Museum. In the entrance they could see the painter Jonas Åkesson's big painting of the officer corps of the Malmo regiment. On the third floor the Museum showed painting and drawings of Carl Fredrik Hill. As a landscape painter he is still unmatched. His drawings under influence of schizophrenia are amazingly creative.

In Jonas Åkesson's home lived the German naval officer Felix von Luckner during his first time in Sweden. During WW1 the German Navy armed the three-mast full rigger Seeadler. For sure a war crime. The ship sailed under false flag as a merchant ship. They went up alongside British merchant ships, showed the cannons and asked the crew to leave the ship, which they then destroyed. The British crews were well taken care of and put ashore in Scandinavia. Finally, the Brits captured von Luckner and imprisoned him in New Zeeland, from where he managed to escape and went to Sweden. By Jonas Åkesson's oldest daughter, living in his home city Dresden, he got in touch with Jonas Åkesson, who welcomed him to stay in his home. Here, the extremely physically strong von Luckner, amused the children by tearing apart phone books and to bend coins between his fingers. After a few years von Luckner met Miss Ingeborg Engeström. They lived in her home at Limhamnsvägen in Malmö, same house as Zlatan bought many years later. von Luckner passed away at Malmo hospital in 1966.

Some Sundays Mona and Sture went to the church at Stadionkyrkan. Not because they were particularly religious, but it was one way to find new acquaintances. And it was closes to their home. Sometimes they took the car and weather permitting they walked the short distance.

They found the house through a real estate agent. The little street it was located on was adorably beautiful during springtime with the blooming Japanese cherry trees. They liked the house from start with the big living room and the big windows towards the garden. The house was located close to a little park and the quite area attracted them. They decided fairy immediately to buy.

One day a lady from the English course entered the shop. She was looking for a dress and Mona could show something that just had arrived. The lady suggested that they should attend a bridge course on Tuesdays, same evening Sture played poker, so that was perfect for Mona. At the bridge course some ladies suggested they should go to a gym, and they found a gym close to Mona's working place.

Among the prison guards the question was if the inmates were human beings. In any case they were of the worst kind. some of them were claiming their "bad childhood", they couldn't manage school, turned addicts and they were stealing to finance their abuse.

Even if Sture was complaining about his work he felt good about it. Which Mona had problems to understand. To be around people you don't appreciate must be hard, but obviously he appreciated his work mates. Her work was kind of creative, while Sture's seemed destructive.

Sture became more and more annoyed over " the bloody immigrants" making problems for the normal taxpayers.

The inmates are not ashamed about what they have done. At least they should be ashamed in front of those close by, and those with children should be ashamed in front of the children. But they don't. The bigger the community they live in the less check they have one each other. Look at Japan. There they commit hara-kiri just because they feel ashamed. What a society. The crueler the crime, the more popular the inmate.

Sometimes I think they get a kick by committing crime. They become someone from being a no one. Maybe it is the same thing with the alcoholics. They get a kick by doing something they didn't dare to do when sober. And next time they have to do something worse to get attention.

Then we have those who get here to live on us. They have to adopt to our way of living. They cannot expect us to adopt to them. Should we break their roles we risk our lives when we visit their countries.

After this monologue Mona realized that it wouldn't be a good idea to invite her girlfriend from Cameroon. She didn't recognize her husband.

Rather soon after Sture's employment they were invited to the manager for the prison guards. Ulf lived with his wife Irene in a luxury apartment on the 6th floor. Irene was a shop assistant like Mona and they immediately found subjects to talk about. It was a pleasant dinner party with only the four of them. Ulf had been a soccer player and they both were happy about MFF, the local soccer team.

- How did you find this profession, Sture wondered.
- I had a photo shop taking very much of my time. then I saw an ad for an employment as a prison guard. I applied and got the job. But this is a few years ago.
- And then you became the managing director.
- Yes, time is passing, and I was in the line to be promoted
- This apartment is really luxury.
- Absolutely perfect for us. We sold our house and got some money. Then we thought an apartment in the middle of the city would be good for us.
- For sure you are well over the sidewalk.
- Yes, the view over the city is good and up here we have light and air.

Sture and Mona carefully avoided subject like politics and religion. That they were Social Democrats weren't anything that they were going to tell. Sture worried about the thank-you-speech after the dinner but Mona praised him for it. Mona had bought a book how to behave at dinners and she gave Sture some hints. We don't touch the food until the hostess says "bon appetit" nor do we touch the wine. We put the silverware on our plates when we don't use them. When the hostess has finished eating, we do the same even if we have food left on our plates. We wrinkle the napkin and put them to the right of our plates to show that we are satisfied with the food. We sit upright without leaning at the backrest of our chairs. And no elbows on the table. At midnight they took a taxi back home.

They were slightly surprised that the host Ulf didn't talk about their work. Sture was newly employed and this was a new world for him. But on the other hand, this was a family dinner. He had been to some introductory courses about violence and escape attempts. As a newly employed he was always accompanied by an experienced colleague. He was learned never to turn his back against an inmate, nor to be alone with an inmate. You never know what the inmate has in mind. And the prison guards weren't their favorites. Which was mutual.

Sture was loyal and he did what he was told. He liked law and order and he was accurate. For sure he didn't want to take risks. No adventures, no gambling, no speculations.

As a former soccer player, he realized the importance of team play. He followed rules and instructions. He appreciated authority. Like all Social Democrats he was basically conservative. He had his opinions and he didn't deviate from them. Maybe a psychiatrist should say he was a guardian character, so the new job was just perfect for him.

His colleagues were nice guys, and many times he wondered why they have chosen this profession. They treated the inmates by distance and even by disrespect. After they had served their sentence the inmates should be released as good citizens.

The prison had 150 inmates. Some serving for murder and others for drug trafficking. Most of the work was to lock in and lock up. The inmates were working at the workshop. They were entitled to one-hour break in the afternoon. For sure it wasn't a burdensome work. The incidents were few. He liked his work. What he didn't like was how his friends or rather his former friend looked down on his new career. For sure it wasn't a status work, but one could make a living on it.

Concerning the incidents, very little happened. Sometimes an inmate argued against the prison guards, Some other time an inmate decided he shouldn't say one single word. That the inmates were fighting between them was rare. This never happened with the professional criminals. They just wanted to get back in business as soon as they possibly could, and not risking an extension of the sentence.

Chapter 5.   Companioship

The recurrence rate for the inmates is about 40%. The reason could be that a good number of them are professional criminals who have problems finding some other occupation.

"One as punishment, one as warning" is an old saying. A more modern view is that the inmate should be integrated into the society. There are as good number of theories how the inmate should be treated. One theory is that he should be isolated in a prison cell with a bible as the only company. Another extreme theory advocates work under silence. The Irish way is isolation with rewards for good behavior. The

Swedish system is work, education and treatment. It looks like Sweden is going for a system with electronic surveillance so the inmate could serve his sentence at home and away from his criminal connections.

The situation in prison is slightly odd. The inmates should be transformed from evil people to good citizens, while the prison guards are transformed from good people to evil. Regarding the prison guard it is against their own intensions.

A good number of the inmates have lower education than average. Nor do they have a permanent work. Only 20% of the inmates were working when convicted compared to 70% of their fellow citizens.

Looking back at the history of imprisonment a lot has happened. And a lot will happen even if we think that we now have the best imprisonment we can get. But that's wrong. The development will go even faster. The view that the punishment is retribution is on its way out. Now we look upon the inmate as a patient who should recover. The problem is to find the right medication for each one of the patients.

The fellowship among the prison guards was good. There was a solidarity and a loyalty Sture appreciated. He felt he was accepted as a good teammate. They socialized even during their spare time. Went to soccer games together, and during summertime they went to the beach together. Mona wasn't too happy about the company, but she brought homemade cookies and did her utmost to be nice and entertaining. Her super body in bikini made Sture's colleagues cockeyed. It wasn't easy for them to keep one eye looking at the one they were talking to and one eye looking at Mona.

If someone of the inmates was critical or oppositional it could happen that the prison guard hit him. Some of the prison guards had a little baton that could spring out from the handle like a spring knife. Strokes on the bare foot blades didn't give bruises. Complaints to the prison management were dismissed as the inmate couldn't show any proof. To report to the Police was useless due to their automatic closures.

The risk for whistleblowers was low. Their friendship was strong, and their characters were weak. That someone would risk his work and the disgust and the mobbing from the colleagues was unlikely. No, the risk was just nonexistent.

The inmates should be grateful for the luxury life they had. A prison is no vacation. The prison guards make sure it isn't. If an inmate asks about a favor, the prison guards refuse just to show their power. Lucifer cannot get further down. However, rapists and pedophiles should be grateful to the prison guards that they survived in prison.

The Lucifer process is rather universal. We have seen the persecutions of non-pure-bred Arians.

A scaring example is when the Germans wanted to get rid a number of prisoners in a concentration camp in Lithuania. They needed 100 men and they asked 120 office workers in Hamburg calculated that 20 would refuse when they understood what the mission was about. All the 120 volunteered to kill the prisoners.

How can a normal human being volunteer for such a mission? Well, the researchers digging into the question have reached the conclusion that those who carry out such a mission they don't look at the "victims" as human beings.

One other example is the Reserve Battalion 101, who, in 1942, killed 1 500 Jewish women, children and elderly. Reserve Battalion 101 was ordinary men too old to do their military service.

The Indian writer Arundhati Roy describes in her book "the God of Small Things" how a wife is treated by her new family. An oppressive prison within the family with a "prisoner" and "prison guards" In the Indian society the woman has to walk 3 steps behind the man. The husband is the one who makes and takes the decisions. Perfect for a Lucifer process.

Maybe it is a universal phenomenon where someone is superior to someone else. In families where the men are commanding and supervising the women.

The discoverer of the Lucifer effect, the social psychologist Philip Zimbardo, claims that the division in "we" and "them" will trigger the process. A good number of experiments show this including an experiment with chimpanzees in Tanzania. However, there is a slight difference between chimpanzees and prison guards. Solely the division in we and them isn't reasonable. There must be more factors. One being power. One other being the fact that the individual with power is looking down upon the one he's exercising his power over. That we get a dichotomy in " we who are more worthy" and "those who are not so worthy". One other factor could be the development of roles within the group with power. On top of that we have the clothing in the prison reinforcing the difference between them and we. In this way the prison is perfect for Lucifer process.

The key word for avoiding a Lucifer process would be equality and consequently that inequal constellations

will trigger a Lucifer process – in
unequal families and groups, in unequal
institutions, societies and cultures, A
horrifying idea.

The Bible nor the Koran are
precisely feministic.

"As in all the churches of the
saints, women should be silent in the
churches. For they are not permitted to
speak, but should be subordinate, as the
law also says. If there is anything they
desire to know, let them ask their
husbands at home. For it is shameful
for a woman to speak in church."
Corinthians 14:34–35

" The woman should be at the
husband's disposal whenever he so
wishes. The woman is like a field
which he could enter whenever he feels
for it" The Koran 2:223, 4:15 and 4:34

" A husband is permitted to beat his
disobedient wife" The Koran 4:34

Charles Dickens is referring to what he calls "'marriage prison guard". " This marriage prison guard keeps his marriage prisoner … in a prison as solid as it was built by iron and granite. A good deal of injustice is committed here than in the most miserable prison. If he's a man with rough desires he's treating his prisoner badly – in the name of the law. The prisoner – the wife – is the belonging of the prison guard …" . Written 200 years ago, but we can imagine the Lucifer effect and the humiliation the wife was exposed to, and in many cases still is exposed to. Maybe, there is a Lucifer effect within the Police force. With their monopoly of violence and the general public as potential criminals – taken care of and still not taken care of. And what about our military institutions? We can continue from institution to institution. The mental institutions were closed down like the institutions for the poor. None of them especially human. Next step should be to close down the prisons. There must be better ways to lead the criminals into a narrower road. Surveillance in the home with GPS close to their families. For the professional criminals there must be other places and other systems.

The Lucifer effect must have been in the history of the humanity as long as homo sapiens has existed. Then we can ask if it has to do with the evolution. That people with power will destroy those they have authority over in the same way as we have the "survival of the fittest". Or is it so that the power people have to have someone they can excess their power over. Without a Fanclub it isn't possible for a fan to survive. Without inmates no prison guards, without criminals no Police. Meaning that the destruction theory isn't applicable.

What creates this evilness that the prison guards are exercising over the inmates? Group pressure and social control are two factors. To surrender the group norms even if you as an individual are of the conviction that the group is wrong. You resign from a personal responsibility. Maybe a personal concealed aggression is revealed. But ahead of all it is the dehumanization of the fellow human beings that makes certain people so cruel. This evilness is a problem when manifested in a tangible cruelness – physical or verbal.

The prison guard in the concentration camps became marvelously cruel. The Jewish – the kapos – and the female were the worst. Maybe the word is originated from the German Kameradenpolizei, maybe not. The kapos were selected among those who were convicted and regarded cruel. Among the female we have Irma Grese

– young and beautiful – and Maria Mandl and Ilse Koch. The training stressed that the prisoners weren't human and, in any case, belonging to a deficient race.

Each and every Lucifer must have a retreat. It is the situation as such that creates the Lucifer effect. Not the personality. Is it so that the effect appears when the person isn't working? At his spare time, at home, when driving. No research has been done about this, but it could be so as there is a change in the personality. A reasonable retreat is to change job.

Maybe the prison guards should get psychiatric treatments to counteract the process. Each prison should have a camera surveillance to check how the prison guards are treating the prisoners.

The civilization in a society is evaluated after how the worst exposed are treated. In each and every society the inmates is an exposed group. Same system with power and someone to have power over. Same personality change when employed as a prison guard. Disregarding where we are in the world.

Normally a personality change appears by psychological interference, a life crisis, or is related to drugs, but in Sture's case it was the employment as a prison guard that triggered his Lucifer syndrome. Maybe he was also affected by the movement to Malmo a new environment and new routines. From a friendly and warm, happy and positive personality to a cold and negative, grumpy and sour. In spite of the fact that he was happy with his new job, the house and with Malmo. In a way he felt happy when an inmate was beaten. Maybe he felt that the prison guard team did something together like in a soccer team.

After some time he realized that many of his colleagues like himself had applied to the Police academy but were turned down. Now they were moonlighting at the dancing halls where they had to be dressed in uniform. Maybe they liked being dressed in a uniform, giving them the personal security, they were missing. The uniform is a power symbol, it designates security and fellowship. At the prison this is very clear, where the prison guards have their nice-looking uniforms, and the inmates theirs not so nice looking. The uniforms designate their roles and how to socialize. Perfect for the Luzifer effect.

In an experiment were the prison guards and the inmates changed roles it was shown that the inmates acquired same kind of cruel behavior as prison guards. Indicating a horrifying system when dividing people in people with power and subordinates.

Just too many released inmates have told about how they were treated in the prison, meaning that the system must be known at the top of the prison management. Or maybe it is the prison management that is affected by the Lucifer syndrome. The cruelties are terrible, but even worse is the indifference.

Chapter 6.   The Revenge

Recommended by the vicar Gustav got an employment as a parking attendant when released. The vicar also managed to find a small apartment for him.

Gustav had to do take a new driver's license. For his savings and some diligence money he bought a worn and torn Golf.

The small house Sture lived in was the first or the last house on a small street. It had a small parking place alongside the house. Behind the house is a park

The car and the house were easily accessible, but it was difficult to approach the house without being notified by the neighbors. During nighttime the little street was well enlightened. He could pretend being a jogger or an advertising distributor like he did when he glued the mailbox with super glue.

The idea was to irritate Sture with pinprick after pinprick. Maybe the pinpricks would create such an irritation for him that he got problems with himself and for the ones close to him.

Best had been if the society had taken its responsibility and punished the prison guards, but now it was like it was and his revenge was the one and only solution. The society had monopoly for punishment, but for revenge the competition is free. However, there were few possibilities. Sture was moving between the home and the prison. Gustav didn't feel for attacking the home. Then the rest of the family may be hurt, and they hadn't done anything wrong. Sture and his wife Mona did some excursions to the tourist attractions around Malmö, but it was impossible to anticipate when and to where. To follow them in his old car he didn't dare to. His car was sticking out just too much.

Phone terror at nights was risky. His phone could be traced. Same way with sending flowers to Sture with the message "From your Darling". With a sufficient amount of money, the flower intermediary would reveal who had sent the flowers. If he was caught and had to serve again it would be even worse.

To get into the parking lot for the prison guards was risky even for a parking attendant. Maybe there was a camera surveillance. But for sure it was tempting to fill the keyhole of his Volvo with Plastic Padding.

Violent pinpricks like crashing windows he didn't feel for.

Sometimes he wondered why not more released inmates did what he planned to do. Maybe they wanted and wished, but it had to be done. It takes energy to take revenge. The prison guards have wives, cars, friends to take revenge on. Some of them also had summer houses and sailing boats.

However, to take revenge on family and friends didn't appeal to Gustav, who had a genuine aversion against violence.

Then he could wonder why he wanted revenge. Maybe to get rid of the feeling of discomfort constantly nagging him. Maybe, it was inborn to have the feeling of revenge for someone who had hurt you. So it wasn't strange that he was trying to figure out how to get his revenge. To forgive was impossible. Like a war veteran he could wake up in the middle of the night cold sweaty after dreaming about the horrors he had experienced remembering the beatings and the verbal accusations. Sometimes he asked himself if he hated Sture. Not really but what he wanted was some kind of rehabilitation for the feeling of inferiority he had in his soul. And of course, he wanted to hurt and to harm him. To hurt and to harm him because he had treated him derogatory.

Sometimes he could ask himself if he was afraid of Sture. But no, it was pure hate. Which he couldn't dream of showing or even indicate. Then Sture may suspect him of the pinpricks he was delivering. No one of the other inmates showed any animosity against the prison guards, but that could be self-protection. What a terrible working place the prison guards have. Could be the reason why they are like they are. Sadistic. Intolerant.

The count of Monte Cristo took revenge on those who got him imprisoned on the island If for 14 years. And he got his merciless revenge.

From the professional criminals Gustav got the impression that they wanted a network where they could feel at home. Kind of a second family. Maybe they didn't think that they could manage an ordinary life. On top of this it looked like that they got a kick from a quick fix. They knew each other from childhood. They had grown up in the same area. They stick together and they have a strong network with an inner circle controlling the network. The nicknames they now have they got already as kids.

When Gustav got released, he had to map how Sture and his family were moving. What kind of hobbies does he have, what are his working hours?

How would Gustav feel after he got his revenge. Liberated? Satisfied? Pleased over what he had achieved? In any case – all the time and resources he spent planning his revenge created some kind of a tie between him and Sture. Hopefully this connection would disappear when he got his revenge so he could continue with his life without Sture hanging over him.

Half an hour before the church service he waited in his car for Sture and Mona. He had waited the Sunday before but then they didn't show up. But today they parked their Volvo at the parking lot and went into the church. Then he drove to their home. In his car he had a parcel and a tube of super glue. At the entrance door he squeezed the tube into the keyhole. The super glue dries in a few seconds and it would take a locksmith to open the door.

Just to be on the safe side he changed the registration number on his car from FGF 951 to EGE 951. Which was easy with some white color. If the neighbors would check the registration number. In case he would be checked by the police he could claim that someone tried to steal his car. He kept the parcel. Could be good to have some other time.

Sture was very punctual. You could set your clock after him. During the summer mornings he had the sun dazzling his eyes. Through a US contact Gustav got a blue laser, imported as green laser.

At a stop light Gustav pretended to check the parked vehicles. If he was lucky Sture had to stop for the red light. Which Gustav could control by pressing the button for walking. When Sture stopped he aimed the blue laser towards his eyes. It must have hurt him as he pulled backwards in his seat.

How should Sture make the connection between his treatment at the prison and Gustav's pinpricks. Well, it had to be solved in one way or another. Maybe he could send a letter written by clippings from the newspaper.

When Sture arrived at the prison he went to see the medical doctor complaining about his eyes.

Mona should pick him up after her work. She took the bus and walked the short way from the bus stop to the prison parking. She went into the car by her set of the car keys. She had never seen the prison this close. What a terrible place, she thought.

- What has happened?
- I don't know. I just got a pain in my eyes when I drove to work this morning.
- What does the doctor say?
- That I have to rest the eyes for a month or two. But he couldn't tell what makes

the pain. So I'm on sick leave for one month.
- Do you have pain somewhere else? Headache?
- No, just in my eyes.
- In any case you could see the car and you can walk without problems. So far so good.
- True
- Let's go home. Close your eys and relax.

Damn, Mona thought, in one way or another I have to remove him from here. Too much has happened during the past year for being coincidences. Is there someone who are making problems with him because he's a prison guard? And I get my share. Who will give a 50-year-old ex-prison guard a job? I have to find a solution. His colleagues are moonlighting at the nightclubs, but that cannot be well paid. We cannot manage on my salary. Office work? He's too young for an early retirement. The banks need guards. Let's see.

BANG! The bang must have been heard over the whole city. A passenger car was blown up at the prison parking lot. A homemade bomb had destroyed one of the passenger cars at the prison parking lot. The car parts landed over the whole parking lot. The bomb was timed at 1715 h but went off at 1700 h. At 1715 the parking lot would have been full of prison guards going home after work. No one was hurt.

Obviously, someone has got the courage to take his revenge, Gustav though. This sign must be obvious for each one of the prison guards. And Sture was at home. I have to arrange for a meeting with him.

Chapter 7. The meeting

About one month after the laser attack Gustav pretended to distribute flyers. It was a beautiful summer day. He rings the doorbell and asks Sture if he could recognize him.
-Yes, even if I cannot see too well right now I recognize you.

Gustav's visit was a break in Sture's rather monotonous days. The small yard didn't require much work. He had put a new parquet floor in the bedrooms. In the hallway he had put a clinker floor. He could do this kind of work in spite of the problems with his eyes.

- Maybe we weren't the best of friends at the prison, tried Gustav.
- Trash and more trash, Sture answered
- Yes, that was how you looked upon us. By the way do I disturb you?
- Disturb and disturb. What do you want?
- Actually nothing. As you see I work as a flyer distributor. There are few jobs an ex-convict can get. And then I saw your name on the mailbox. We met almost every day for 2 years and now I almost miss you.
- Haha, I don't think you miss me too much.
- What happened to your eyes?
- I don't know. All of a sudden when I was driving to work I felt a pain. The medical doctor at the prison thought that I should be on sick leave for a month and that is what I'm doing right now.

- Maybe you are stressed and overworked, Gustav answered.

This was a strange coincidence. That the mailbox said Wilhelmsson didn't necessarily mean that it was him who lived here. On the other hand, if he was distributing flyers, he could have seen him some other time. He knew Gustav as a friendly man, always with a smile on his face. He got very few visitors even if this visitor was unexpected.

- I was going to have a cup of coffee. Please, join me if you aren't in a hurry
- A cup of coffee would be nice.

They sat down at the table in the small garden. Alongside the wall to the house next to Sture's there was a flowerbed of roses.

- Do you have any contact with the other ones released, Sture tested.
- Absolutely not. The vicar, who helped me with a job, said that I should stay away from the released inmates. The

contact I had with them was merely on the other side of the table tennis table.
- Yes, you played a lot and you went to Stockholm. Talking about the vicar he's a reasonable man and not especially vicarious. It was nice of him to help you. Do you keep in contact with him?
- No, but as some kind of appreciation I attend his church service from time to time.

This went far better than Gustav could have dreamed of.
- For how long have you lived here?
- For about three years
- It's a quiet place with lots of green areas.
- Oh yes, we really like it here
- What about your work? Do you also like what you are doing?
- Very, very good. I was working in an office before, but this is more enjoyable
- Aren't you worried about that someone newly released will recognize you when

you go shopping or when go to a soccer
game?
- That's something I never have thought
about. Work is one thing and leisure
time is another. I don't even think that
the professional criminals even should
say hello if we met.
- No, they are frequent guest and as a
guest you have to show the host some
respect. Haha.
- Most of them move back to their homes
all over the country so the risk is low.
It's not free of charge to attack an
official.
- That's right. The buns are excellent.
Have you baked them yourself?
- We buy them at a confectionary in the
city.

It was important for Gustav
to create some kind of trust before he
could indicate a connection between the
pinpricks and the treatment he got at the
prison. Maybe the laser in his eyes was

too much, but anyway. Now it was done.
- Do you go to church? The vicar's church is very close from here.
- Oh yes, we go the church located close to Stadion.
- Are you active in the church?
- No, it is more of a habit since childhood. It started with Sunday school.
- It looks like we both are from Smaland. From Vastervik judging from your accent.
- Yes, that's correct and what about you?
- Not far from there. I guess you know where Hultsfred is located.
- That's where I met my wife Mona at a public dancing hall.
- And now we both live in Malmo.
- Do you intend to remain in Malmo?
- Malmo is more exciting than Hultsfred. How do you like Malmo?
- The city as such is perfect if it hadn't been for the citizens. Haha.

- You mean the southern drawl?
- Since we moved in here it has been problems with a lot of things. When Mona went shopping someone cut off the valve on our front tire. And someone glued the lid on our mailbox, and someone. put glue in the keyhole to our front door. We have too many immigrants in Malmo.
- Then you have been innocently attacked.
- What could we possibly have done to them?
- And you don't think someone want to take revenge?
- For what?
- Well, once you squeezed my fingers in the door to the cell. And once you stepped on my foot.
- Nothing I recall. Would you like to take revenge?
- I believe the vicar that you have to forgive. Do you have anyone you suspect?

- In that case it should be all those in for the first time.
- Then you have a quite a selection to choose from. Many times, I wondered why you took such terrible care of us. According to your instructions as a prison guard we should have got a totally different treatment.
- Those who are interned are the trash of the society. The real bottom. They don't deserve anything else. Just imagine how much tax money we could have saved if we had a death penalty. The Muslims should be halal slaughtered. The penalties are far too low, and the inmates live far too comfortably. For many of them it is a way to get food and shelter.
- Two weeks ago, a passenger car was blown up at the prison parking lot. Do you think someone wanted revenge?
- I read about that, but that day a gang member was to be released, and I think the rivaling gang took the wrong car.

- Yes, maybe that's the way it was.
- It's very good that they are killing each other. The sooner we get rid of them the better.
- The prison management must have noticed how you treated us. Their responsibility is that we are released as lawful citizens, working and paying our taxes.
- Yes, that cannot have escaped them.
- But that's not the way it works in practice. The criminal authority is like politicians. They say one thing and they do something else. And who cares?
- Are you watching the soccer games at Stadion?
- It happens, but my wife Mona isn't interested so I have to go with the colleagues or alone.
- It looks like MFF will win this year as well.
- So it looks
- Do you have children?

- We have a daughter studying at Lund University.
- And you have to attend classes for prison guards. Could be a nice break from the daily routine.
- Yes, the criminal authorities are trying to find a solution for the professional criminals.
- Have they found the formula?
- A working community for them like the vicar got you a job and a place to live.
- Yes, that must be the formula. There are a good number of organizations voluntarily working in this direction.
- What kind of profession did you dream of as a child?
- A Police Officer. It looked exciting to catch criminals. And what about you?
- Having a construction company like my father.
- You served for drunk driving? But what did you do?
- I took a border truck and drove around the factory area a Saturday evening.

- Maybe that wasn't the worst of crimes. That was also what the police back in Hultsfred said when they contacted us.
- Yes, and it looks like what the factory owners also thought. If I begged on my bare knees, I think they would let me work for them again.
- Is that what you want?
- Not really. The label is there – The Alcoholic. Terrible for my parents. I like Malmo. Working as a flyer distributor isn't spiritually elevating and then I have a job as parking attendant. – thanks to the vicar.
- I wish that many first-time offenders could get the backing you have got. When it comes to the professional criminals, I really don't know what to do with them. Only to make their time in prison such a hell they don't want to come back. The smart ones are planning crimes that they sell to other criminals.

Even if Sture didn't suspect him of all his problems he wanted to give him a hint. But how?
- If you excuse me. I would like to rest my eyes for a while. But we can keep talking.
- I guess the doctor wanted you to rest your eyes.
- Yes, that was his recommendation.
- Wouldn't it be good for you to wear sunglasses?
- I haven't thought about that. Thank you.

Sture leaned back in his chair and closed his eyes. Now he feels confident, Gustav believed. But how to give him a hint that the attacks are a revenge?

- Maybe you don't want to talk about the prison?
- It is perfectly all right. In the same way you say you miss me, I miss my work and my colleagues. The prison

management sent me flowers, which I really appreciated. But no one has visited me yet. I guess that we all have our own things to think about.

- That's the way it is. Why not separate the first-time criminals from the professionals?
- You mean to have separate institutions for them
- Exactly.
- In a way we already have that. The drunk drivers we usually have in some kind of open institution with treatment. They are also working in the profession they had when they were taken care of.
- But that isn't the way it is at our prison.
- I guess it is a question of resources. Weren't you ever contacted by the professionals?
- I guess I looked too stupid for that.
- Haha. We have to solve the problem with the relapse. Almost 50% of them are back within two years and within three years 70% are back.

- Do you have any ideas what to do about it?
- Double the penalties. The shorter the time they are free the less time they have to make problems for ordinary citizens.
- Maybe you can send them to Siberia?
            Which Gustav said as a joke.
- Absolutely and where it is the coldest. Most important is to keep them separated. The only thing they think about is how to get money.
- The prison is a perfect place to meet other criminals.
- Yes, and at the prison they have some kind of a home with order and care and they get good food at regular times.
- Many of the inmates have children and then it is extra problematic to serve a punishment.
- They should have thought of that before the committed the crime.
- Or before they got children.

- For many of them it is hard to change career.
- That's exactly what they are supposed to do.
- What do you think of letting the first-time offenders serve the sentence at home with some kind of surveillance?
- Stupidity. Then they can walk in and out as they please. They have committed a crime and they should serve for that.
- The contact with the professionals isn't good nor the environment. You feel hateful against the society and against the personnel.
- Do you feel hateful?
- I cannot deny that. And humiliated as a human being.
- I have never talked about this before,
- For such a conversation should work we have to be on the same level. Not as prison guard and prisoner. And without uniforms.
- The inmates have no uniforms.

- They don't have their own personal clothes but are dressed in funny looking clothes. The prisoners have their dignity, and their integrity.
- I've never thought about that.
- And you as prison guards are dressed as a better kind of human beings.
- Sounds like a theatre. Haha.
- Yes, like a theatre. With your uniform you play your role and I play my role in my uniform. Without uniforms we play different roles in the prison theatre. The world is like a theatre – we all play our roles. Which I read somewhere.
- In the uniform you feel different than without.
- Do you like your uniform?
- Yes, in fact I do.
- I have heard that in the US prisons the inmates are wearing blue jeans and a jacket.
- Perhaps we should consult a fashion designer. Haha.

- Maybe I disturb you for too long. But it is fun to talk to you.
- - You don't disturb. It is kind of boring to stay home. And I cannot drive a car. But maybe you want to distribute your flyers?
- The mailboxes are open around the clock, so I'm not in a hurry. My work as a parking attendant starts at 8 am.
- Do you want more coffee?
- .- Yes, please. When do you think you an start working again?
- For Christmas I should be fully recovered.
- Good to hear. When in prison I wondered why I personally was punished and not for the crime I did.
- How do you mean?
- What I did was of course terrible, And that is what I should be punished for. Not me as a human being
- Tricky. I don't understand.
- What I'm trying to do is to separate me as a human being and the crime.

- We are all delivered as a parcel and we cannot sort out good and bad in this parcel.
- We can take out the crime as such and admit we have done something wrong. And be punished for that.
- Could you, please, give me some more coffee?
- A full cup or half a cup? How many lumps of sugar do you want?
- Half a cup. I have sugar already. Haha
- Talking about inmates. The friends and the relatives to the victims want revenge. Take Annika Östberg. Her boyfriend committed murder. For sure the victims are of the opinion that even she should be punished.
- The US authorities had to smuggle her out.
- Yes, I think most people were of the opinion that she had served just too long time for her part in the murder.

- For people who are sick in their heads,
the prison isn't the right place. They
should be cured at a mental hospital
- Right, that kind of people we don't
want. And those who have caused
financial damage should pay those who
have been damaged.
- Financially they should be crippled for
lifetime.
- And then Sibiria.
- Maybe it could be a good idea for the
criminals to meet the ones they have
hurt.
- Do you really think they care?
- Maybe, maybe not. But it will be hard
for him to neglect a person in front of
him showing his damages.
- Hard to believe.
- In any case it would be good if the
perpetrator can realize that he has hurt
someone else.
- You have been thinking about this quite
a lot.

- Well, I had some time to think as an inmate.
- Do you have more ideas?

That Gustav was of the opinion that the prisons should be closed down and permanently, he couldn't tell Sture. In any case it was possible to talk to Sture and he had got his revenge. He didn't regret what he had done to Sture.

- It looks like you already at the day care center can see who will be a criminal. Children who are violent. To take care of them already at that stage.
- Do your really believe in that?
- Could be something to think about.
- Except for separating the professional criminals from the other inmates. I think you should treat the ones in for first time and the permanent guests differently.
- To separate those really established in the business and those on their way. Haha

- Perhaps it is possible to save a few.
  Most of them are just tools for the big
  boys. Then, I think it is important for
  the prison guards to show respect for
  the inmates, so they feel they are part of
  the society. A cog in the machinery.
- But in the wrong machinery. Haha.
- Then we have the pedophiles. It doesn't
  help to cut off their cocks. The problem
  is in their heads. They should be cured
  at a mental hospital.
- Then you'll empty the catholic church.
  Haha
- There I fully accept your opinion halal
  slautered. Children confined to adults
  should be safe. Talking about revenge.
  Which revenge do the abused children
  take as adults?

Gustav felt that this had
worked much better than he could
dream of. Face to face it was possible to
talk to Sture. Maybe he'll get more
opportunities.

\- You wondered if I have more ideas. Perhaps the inmates could work at a construction site with full salary. Then they would have a good deal of money when released and they have got more contacts. Then they won't have the same intension to find money when released.

\- That's no punishment. For someone who doesn't have a work it is a reward.

\- Could be one way away from criminality.

\- We can never cure the trash.

\- Maybe, but if we don't try, we'll never succeed.

\- That's' true.

\- What do you think we should do?

\- I really don't know. Could be that part of the society is trash and will so remain.

\- Genetically, you mean?

\- In many cases it looks like it is hereditary

- If that was the case it would be dreadful, but it looks like the genome is different and specific for the brutal criminals.
- You have done your homework. Haha.
- Yes, I have had plenty of time. You have to break the networks. The professionals know each other from childhood and the network is like their family.
- Yes, that's obvious at the prison.
- It cannot be too difficult to map the networks and to split the criminals in each and every network.
- Good idea, which I'll forward to the prison management. Maybe you should put your ideas in writing on a piece of paper.
- Do you think they care?
- We do all we can to reduce the relapses. They are responsible for the main part of the crimes. With a good formula the politicians will listen.

- What would you like to do if you were in charge?
- Lock them in for good. The professionals shouldn't have their freedom. Same thing with fighting dogs.
- Sounds dramatic.
- It's a small part of the professionals who commit the main part of the crimes. Kind of 80/20-rule. This group cannot be too hard to map and to observe.
- The inmates I met in prison were like just anybody, but when they are released, they know what to do. Surveillance with GPS should be of great help.
- They want to be released and that's why they behave well in prison.
- You mean that after being convicted for the third time they should be locked up for good.
- Yes, that's my opinion.

-   Some of them have better lawyer than others.
-   Sure, but the main rule is obvious.
-   Now I have to leave. Thanks for the coffee and the talk. Get well. I'll find my way out.

Well, Gustav concluded, maybe Sture got something to think about. Hopefully I won't see him again. Now I can put all this behind me. He slept better than he had done for a long time. Revenge is liberating.

Chapter 8.   Securitate

Sture went more and more into his own circles. The work, the poker evenings, and the soccer games at Malmo Stadion. Then he worked on the house, especially when he was on sick leave.

Mona felt they were drifting apart from each other. She also felt some kind of emotional distance from Sture. The passion wasn't like before. When they met Sture could play bedroom Bingo so she could scream Bingo after the 5th orgasm in a row. Now it was long time between the moments.

Even Mona went into her circles. The English course, the bridge evenings, the gym and her work.

She understood she was appreciated by her boss. And for sure she was able to separate the customers from their money. The shop owner gave her clothes from the latest collection and she felt the eyes when she walked in the city.

Obviously, her appearance in the city had an impact on the number of customers visiting the store. The customers trusted her advice. A new kind of clientele came. Those who wanted the latest and were willing to pay for it.

The shop owner wanted Mona to be present when the sellers showed the collection for the next season. It was kind of survival for the store to choose the right collection and to sell all of it during the season. What was left they had to sell to secondhand stores for close to nothing. A dress for say $ 500 they had to dump for $ 5. That's the way it is with fashion.

She worried about Sture. The prison wasn't good for him. From a friend she had heard that Securitas was looking for new employees. But how to convince him. Old fashioned as he was. Maybe she could invite her friend and her husband for dinner.

Sture was happy for the guests and for the dinner party. He bought entrecote, which he marinated in coffee and HP sauce. For dessert he bought green cheese and as a starter they should have herring and vodka.

He put a white cloth on the Gripsholm table, and he set the table with plates and cutlery. Red wine for the meat and also for the cheese.

The guests arrived at 1900 h sharp. They lived just a few blocks away. Elisabeth and her husband

Christer. Christer was rather newly employed by Securitas.

- What about some gin and tonic, Sture asked.
- Yes, please, answered Christer. But be careful with the tonic. Just let the bottle sweep over the gin. A slice of lemon would be nice.
- Sure. And what about Elisabeth?
- Some more tonic than Christer.
- Maybe like me and Mona 2 centiliters of gin and 3 centiliters of tonic with lemon.
- Perfect!
- Cheers and good to see you here.
- Thank you and we are very happy for being here.
- How long have you lived here?
- About four years now
- I can see that you have a Scanian pennant in the flagpole.
- Well, we look upon it as a Smalandian pennant. Same colors - red and yellow.

- Then Smaland and Scania have something in common.
- Does Christer want wormwood spiced vodka or Vodka Special to the herring?
- If you have wormwood spiced vodka, I would love that. You have to get used to it before you appreciate it. And it should have room temperature. Only bad quality vodka should be ice cold to hide the taste
- I fully agree with you. It is the same with beer. If served ice cold you cannot fell the taste. And what about Elisabeth?
- I prefer Vodka Special
- Bon appetite!

Mona and Elisabeth discussed fashion. Why can't you have two fashions at the same time? It looks like the more expensive the new dresses are the more they sell. Same way with perfume. Maybe the customers want to show that they can afford the new collection. And you cannot sell two identical dresses. Each and every customer wants to be unique.

- We don't have that kind of problems. During my working hours I have my uniform and during my leisure time I wear blue jeans. I guess it is the same with you Sture.
- Yes, sure.

That Sture didn't like blue jeans was his secret. Blue jeans were for farmhands and he didn't want to identify with them.

- Where have you bought the herring? This is not Abba.
- From the fishermen when they arrive in the morning.
- Super
- May I serve you another piece of herring.
- Absolut. Or wormwood. Haha
- Both then
- You work at the prison if I understand Elisabeth correctly.

- I have been there for four years now.
- The it is time for a change. Three years on the first job and then five on the next one. Good for the salary.
- And you work for Securitas as I understand Mona.
- Yes, and we need more personnel. With the experience you have, you will be just perfect for us.
- Is it correct that Securitas is a subsidiary to Ceausescu's' Securitate.
- Haha, for sure. The Swedish one.
- The meat is super. How did you manage?
- Oh thank you. Marinated in coffee for three days. Then I have baked it in the oven and then fried it.
- Coffee marinated. Never heard of.
- That works and with some spices and HP sauce. Our daughter Anna who is studying at the Lund University told us that that she is running a big computer and she get the result in a split second.

- Nowadays there are machines for everything. Washing machines, baking machines, and God knows what.
- Pretty soon we can rest in the hammock and just watch the machines working for us.
- The development has gone very quickly, and it will go even quicker. Now there are even computers for private persons in their homes.
- Yes, but the computer guru Bill Gates claims that a private person doesn't need more than 3 kilobites whatever that can be.
- This is a very luxury wine. Where have you found is?
- We visit a liquor store in Denmark. This is a Rioja named Equador which we like very much.
- I'll remember that. Should I check if you can start working for us? For sure you'll get a higher salary than you now have.
- Please, do.

Mona didn't know if she should laugh or cry. This worked better than she had imagined.

- What about some cheese? It has turned really green after three months in the fridge
- Let's give it a try. Oh dear, this is an Italian Gorgonzola.
- Yes, this is our favorite. It walked home all by itself. Haha.

The Rioja and the Gorgonzola was a perfect match. The Gorgonzola was served with crisp bread.

- Cheers Mona and Sture and thank you for an excellent dinner and a wonderful company. I'll do all I can so we can be colleagues.

Half a year later Sture was employed by Securitas. In the beginning he was working daytime. During nighttime it could be good to have a dog. A lady in Lund had got a stroke and she couldn't take care of her extremely well-trained German shepherd – a light brown dog with fairly long hair. He could do a number of tricks like playing "dead dog", be ashamed dragging his paw over his nose. He was a pleasant company during the night routes.

Mona noticed that Sture had changed. He was calmer and not that critical against the immigrants. Maybe she could invite Alice.

She told Sture about Alice and said that she really wanted them to invite her. Maybe Sture know someone they could invite as well.

- Not someone I can think of right now.
- You had someone here when you were on sick leave.
- Gustav. Oh yes. He's nice but how to find him? But God damn it, the vicar must have his phone number. I'll call the vicar on the double.

Alice came from the French part of Cameron. She was the youngest of seven siblings. Her father remarried a substantially younger woman when his first wife died giving birth to their third child. Her mom escaped a number of times from her elderly husband, but after the first child she stayed. He was a good man for her and she had a good life.

Fruit was growing in abundance and fruit was the main food for the family.

Alice entered the nursing school. Studying was easy for her and a few years later she had her exam.

Her elderly brother had moved to Massif Central in France and he suggested that Alice should work as a nurse in France. Better salary and more possibilities. Now it wasn't as easy as her brother imagined. The French hospital required a French nursing exam. However, she could work as an assistant nurse. That solved her contemporary needs.

Her French nurse exam she could take at the hospital which also was University hospital. With a good head she had her French nurse exam in one year.

In Massive Central she meets Alf, who is working as a guide for the Swedish tourist company Intersol. He asks the adorable beauty for direction.

- May I call you if I need another address?
- You can always give it a try.

Alf is a good-looking man and very charming, so Alice gives him her phone number.

During his next trip Alf wanted to have dinner with Alice.

Except for being a stunning beauty she's entertaining and social. After two bottles of wine it wasn't difficult to get her into bed. She has a super body, tall and slender. with a big bosom and a slim waist.

Alf is calling Alice from every phone he come across. He gets Alice's working hours, so he knows when to call her.

This feels good for both of them and when the tourist season is over with Alice moves in with Alf in Lund.

Alice has to attend the compulsory language course in Swedish SFI – Scanian for Immigrants. After half a year they can communicate in Swedish.

In Lund Alice has the same problem with the Nursery School. Now she has to take the exam in Swedish. Bright as she is she manage even this. Now she has no less than three Nursery exams.

Between the tourist seasons Alf is working as a door-to-door salesman for a vacuum cleaner company. Ten knocks and two thanks is his aim and that works. Financially they have a good life.

The charming and good-looking Alf sells not only vacuum cleaners, he's also selling himself. Lots of horny housewives are getting laid. Why he couldn't make Alice pregnant is a good question.

One day Alf doesn't come back home. He has moved in with a lonely lady. Leaving Alice.

Gustav was surprised when the vicar called and asked if he could give his phone number to Sture. He was equally surprised when Sture called and invited him for dinner. What was this all about? Did Sture suspect anything? He calmed down when Sture told him that he wasn't working for the prison any longer.

- It will be a pleasure. Time and dress?
- At 1830 h this coming Friday.
- Who else is invited?

- Mona's classmate Alice. She's from Africa somewhere.
- Sounds exciting.

And for sure it was an exciting evening. The generally rather silent Sture was in an excellent mood. He loved his new job at Securitate, as he called the company. The dog was constantly by his side and he could show the tricks for the guests.

The menu was the same one as they had when Elisabeth and Christer visited them.
- How do you know each other, Alice wondered.
- Gustav gives us parking tickets, Sture answered immediately.

When the cheese was served, Alice took very little and she ate close to nothing.
- Don't you like cheese, Mona questioned
- Even if I eat everything, there are certain things I eat very little of.

- I'll check the fridge, I think we have a mango in there.
- Yes, I can take that.
- Haha. You have really learnt Scanian. We who have lived north of Scania we say "yes, please"
- I never thought of that.
- It's the same in the shop where I'm working. The customers say " I take that and that".
- How did you end up in Lund?

Then Alice had to tell her story how she met Alf, and how she met Mona at a language course in English.

Gustav was fascinated of the dark beauty with catching giggle and the outclass humor.

Mona could understand that Alice's favorite color was black. Black slacks and a black jumper.

- Come and see me at the shop, you'll get my discount.
- Maybe some day

- What do you do during your spare time?
- As you know there is a shortage of nurses, so I have to work a lot. But I'm interested in quiz.
- The soccer fan club has a quiz every Sunday during the summer, if that could be something for you.
- Sounds great. At what time?
- They start at eleven. It is a nice walk around the Baltic park. If you are free, we can see each other at the amphitheater around eleven.

Both Mona and Sture was surprised that Alice had accepted so quickly. But good if they could find each other. That there would be a baptizing at Petri church a year later no one of them could imagine.

- There aren't many colored people in Malmo.
- What? Colored? I'm born like this.

And Alice was laughing her catching laugh.

- It isn't easy to enter the dancing halls. The guards claim you are drunk and then you are barred. Strange that it is only we dark skinned who are drunk.
   Sture thought about his former colleagues. That they are making problems for the guest's - racists as most of them are.
   Sture told that he was interested in healthy food. More fruit and less meat. Alice said that her family in Africa lived on fruit and almost fruit only.
- How do you know Mona? Gustav wondered.
- We attend the same course in English.
- I thought that every African speak English
- Cameroun, where I come from, was a French colony, and it is the same in all the former French colonies, there they speak French, and top of the local languages.
- What about yourself?

- Some English and some German, but
you are better in Scanian than I am.
        Sture tried to find a subject
that could be interesting for all of them.
Regarding soccer Mona had the opinion
that it was stupid to see 22 adults
running after a small ball.
- What would you do if you won a
million on the lottery?
- I would retire in Cameroon. Lay down
on the beach and just relax.
- And what about Gustav?
- I would buy a taxi or two.
- Do you think it is a profitable
operation?
- Maybe not, but then I will be my own
manager.
- And Mona?
- I would buy shares for all the money.
Same shares as Rockefellers and then I
would be as rich as they are.
- And what about yourself Sture?
- I would pay the debts on the house.
More like an insurance if Mona or I

would be incapable of working. Or buy a sailing boat.
- Alice nor Gustav want to buy a house?
- I have a condominium in Lund and that is good for me.
- I have a tenancy here in Malmo and that is perfect for me. It is like living in a hotel. If there are problems the landlord fixes it. Otherwise you have to be a builder and a gardener. Which you must have noticed Sture?
- True. The lawn must be cut and the flower beds have to be cleaned from weed.

At 11 pm Alice and Gustav took a taxi. Gustav heading for his apartment and Alice for Malmo C to take the train to Lund.
- Aren't you afraid of going by train this late a Saturday evening?
- Of course, I am. A screaming gang of youngsters can do just anything. And they aren't color blind.
- Stay in my apartment overnight.

- If I may I would be grateful. I have everything I need in my two handbags.

This was the prelude for a life long relationship. At the Sunday quiz they won a flower check. They enjoyed the crossword puzzles in the local newspaper.

They lived in Gustav's apartment, but after some time they moved to Alice's bigger apartment in Lund.

Epilogue

Mona got her Sture back. She couldn't understand how his personal transformation had occurred, but she realized it had to do with his work as a prison guard. She wasn't familiar with the Lucifer effect. In any case Sture was his old self - positive and joking and less aggressive to the immigrants. Alice influenced him. Her relaxed way of living had Sture's full sympathy.

She also managed to win Karl's sympathy. Karl didn't like colored people. The winters in Chicago could be very cold despite the big lakes.

When a construction project was finished the construction workers had to get rid of material that could be used as fuel. When they offered the blacks to take care of the material for the winter, they said that now it is summer and now we don't need any fuel.

Like most Swedish descendants he voted for the republicans. His conservative opinion followed him back in Sweden and at the Swedish elections.

The first born was baptized Carl Gustav Styrbjörn in Petri church with Mona and Sture as baptismal witnesses. They were also wedding witnesses at Malmo courthouse, with the double doctor, Professor Christos Tsiparis, as wedding officiator. He was temporarily in Malmo for a short break as his work in Cologne where he, together with seven other specialists, tried to solve the mystery of the hieroglyphs. Christos gave a warm speech for the newlyweds at the wedding dinner at the restaurant at Malmo courthouse.

The house right opposite Mona's and Sture's was for sale. Sture gave Gustav a hint. Alice sold her apartment in Lund and the money she got was sufficient for the bank to give them credit for the rest of the payment.

Two years after Carl was born Christina Jelo arrived. Christina was a strong-willed young lady. If she didn't want to sleep, she didn't. And she screamed until she was taken into the parent's bedroom. Carl could be brought to sleep by checking for a peacock on the roof. Christina didn't buy that trick.

Karl visited them to take care of Christina when she was screaming at night. He carried Christina on his shoulder where she slept.

Christina had her peculiarities. There is a test for three-year olds to check their development. Alice went to the childcare center no less than three times. Christina refused to do the tests. Can't you try Alice asked Gustav.

Christina was asked to button a button in a cardigan. Which she did very quickly and throwed the cardigan to the doctor. Then they wanted her to walk on a plank. She jumped on one leg. The doctor wrote in his journal that "Christina has very good contact with her father" implicitly meaning she has not so good contact with her mother. With the result that the Social Security ended up in the house to check the mother. Alice had a good laugh.

Christina and dentists was an extraordinary story. Alice went with her to almost all dentists in Malmö, but the stubborn Christina refused to open her mount. If she did it was for biting the dentist. Gustav complained about this at work. The secretary's husband was working as a dentist. He suggested that Gustav brought Christina after the work hours. The dentist, dressed in casual clothes, wanted to anaesthetize. Christina looked suspicious.

- Try on my arm

Christina injects the needle in the dentist's arm. Surprised over what she had done she opens her mouth and the tooth was out.

Another time she asked Gustav:

- Do you scream when you go to the dentist?
- No
- I do

And for sure she did. When the dentist had finished, all of a sudden she was calm and quiet and asked:

- May I have a toy now?

A sunny Sunday Alice and Sture and the dog took a long walk down to the marina. Malmo had, and maybe still has, the biggest yacht harbor in Sweden. A sailing boat salesman showed them a 6,5 m long sailing boat. Which is about 22 feet. They bought the boat convinced that both Gustav and Mona would accept their decision. Even two of the neighbors wanted to be sailboat owners. None of them had time for sailing so it was good. Now they were four families sharing the boat. On top of the fact that sailing is like being in an ice cold shower tearing 1000 dollar notes into pieces.

Their Ohlsson 22 was a perfect boat for a family. Easy to sail and spacious for its size. For Sture, who wanted to sail single handed, she wasn't the best of boats as she couldn't be sailed on the main sail only. Consequently, he argued for a boat that could be sailed on the main sail only and a few years later the families agreed to buy a 12,5-meter-long sailing boat. More speed and more space.

There were many very pleasant summer vacations on the boats for the four neighbors.
Parents know that the first-born child is taken better care of than the second born. They measure and they put the child on a scale to see the development. They read fairy tales for the first born and try to make it read and count. It was the same thing with Carl and Christina.
During a sailing vacation Christina grabs one of Carl 's books and asks "what's the meaning of this word?" "and this word?" Back home she could read. Later in life it was obvious that she has inherited her mother's aptitude.

Through Sture Alice and Gustav was invited to Sture's colleagues at Securitas. Alice was good at parties with her cheerful personality. Kind of a celebrity she became when she took part in a quiz program on TV.

Securitas was looking for someone who could install surveillance cameras. Sture and his colleagues recommended Gustav for this position. Now the former enemies were not only neighbors and friends, but also colleagues.

Gustav realized and he understood the Lucifer effect and thus he could see Sture as two different persons.

During his time as an inmate he wanted his revenge and then forget about Sture. But that also means that there is no reconciliation. Kind of escapism and the bitterness will remain. In the same way the bitterness will remain when one of the conflicting persons wants reconciliation but the other person refuses. Unforgiveness as revenge.

We have seen that conflicts can be solved just prior to death, which is liberating for the survivors.

Enemies are persons, states and even cultures, who want revenge for what they see as unfairness in the past. It is obvious that it is not easy, and maybe even impossible, to find a reconciliation in conflict that has implied incredible sufferings and even an evil sudden death. Reconciliation doesn't necessarily mean forgiveness. It is totally unthinkable that the survivors from Srebrenica, Rwanda, Siberia or from the concentration camps should forgive.

Willingness to find reconciliation is based on shared interests in one way or another. Without shared interests there is no reason for hostility. The hostility as such is a sign of shared interests. That there is some kind of contact between the conflicting sides. It is these shared interests that opens up for a dialogue.

The Icelandic poem Havamal has a stanza about friends and enemies which is to the point.

> "My friend is my friend
> and so is my friend's enemy.
> but not my enemy's friend."

Indicating you have to be careful who is your friend and who is not. In this specific case the earlier enemies Sture and Gustav could make friends and even good friends. But what about the general case? God and Lucifer are enemies reflecting the conflict between good and bad. They cannot make friends. They have a permanent and eternal conflict.

Then the question is how to proceed from animosity to

reconciliation? For sure a tricky question. How to formulate a theory of reconciliation?

One factor in such a theory is justice. Each one of the parties have their view of what is justice, and then – like the verdict in court - there is a third justice, a more objective one that the parties have to agree upon sooner or later.

One other factor is equality. That the two parties are fairly equal, equally strong, financially equal, socially equal, equal power. If not, the stronger one will have his justice.

A third factor is trust. If an agreement is reached, how can the parties trust that the agreement is followed.

In the case of Sture and Gustav the Lucifer effect turned everything upside down. As we have discussed earlier there could be a good number of cases where Lucifer is working, characterized by inequality.

Another factor is communication. That the parties can talk to each other. Either directly or through a third party.

Still another factor is time. That the parties can end the conflict before it has escalated. It is doubtful that time heals all wounds.

In many cases it not a question of forgiveness but to get your peace of mind.

How is it possible to reduce the inequalities we have in families, groups, institutions, societies and cultures? Maybe through a Lex Lucifer paying attention to the problem. And treatments for the prison guard especially, but also for other personnel in hierarchies showing indications of the Lucifer effect.